Contents

MW01528853

The iPod.. 1
The iPod mini....................................... 2
Charging the Battery (AC adapter).......... 3
Charging the Battery (via the Dock)....... 4
Getting songs onto your computer........ 5
Importing songs from a music CD 6
The iTunes Music Store 7
Downloading songs from the Internet....8
Playing a song in iTunes 9
Which song is playing right now........... 10
Changing a song's name in iTunes 11
Creating your own iTunes playlists....... 12
Sorting music in iTunes 13
Deleting songs from iTunes...................... 14
Deleting an entire playlist......................... 15
Ranking your songs...................................... 16
Creating Smart Playlist in iTunes 17
Naming your iPod... 18
Getting songs into your iPod.................... 19
How to turn your iPod on and off 20
The Thumb Wheel and Select Button.. 21
Using the Thumb Wheel............................ 22
Playing a song on your iPod 23
Pausing the currrent song 24
Fast fowarding or skipping a song.......... 25
Scrubbing through a song.......................... 26

Adjusting the volume................................... 27
Getting back to the Main Menu............ 28
Playing your playlists................................... 29
Playing songs in random order 30
Playing the same song over and over.... 31
Creating On-The-Go playlists 32
Finding songs by browsing........................ 33
Putting your iPod to sleep 34
How much battery time is left 35
Saving your battery power 36
Turning on the backlight............................ 37
How long the backlight stays on 38
Customizing the Main Menu 39
Updating the songs on your iPod.......... 40
Balancing the volume between songs... 41
Setting the time on your iPod 42
How to set an alarm...................................... 43
Turning off the click sound 44
Setting the built-in EQ 45
How many songs can you add................. 46
Setting your LCD screen contrast 47
Playing the iPod's built-in games 48
Deleting a song from your iPod.............. 49
If your iPod won't turn on 50
Where to find iPod accessories 51
Index... 52

Learn the iPod for 5 Bucks

Stephen Gregory

Fair Shake Press, an imprint of Pearson Technology Group, division of Pearson Education

Composed in the typeface Cronos MM from Adobe Systems

ISBN 0-321-28785-1

9 8 7 6 5 4 3 2 1

Printed and bound in the United States of America

"Yeah, I'd pay five bucks to learn more about that...."

How to use this book

Welcome to a new way of learning about cool high-tech products. This book is different than others because it has just one goal: to get to the fun part. I have to admit up front that I'm not to teach you everything about the iPod. That's right, you're not going to learn the difference between AAC encoding and MP3 encoding, and I'm not going to talk about audio bit-depth or transfer rates, and all that other boring stuff. If you wanted to learn all that, you'd have bought a $40 iPod book.

Nope, you bought this book because you're the kind of person who doesn't need to know all the techno-geek stuff about the underlying technology—what makes an iPod tick—instead you just want to start using your iPod today. You want to learn how to do all the cool things like sorting and organizing your songs, creating your own playlists, and getting tracks from your computer onto your iPod so you can get to really important stuff—the music. That's what this book is all about. I cover only the most requested, most important, and most useful aspects of the iPod so you can start having fun with it right away.

Now, since there are two different iPods (the original iPod and the newer iPod mini) I had to cover them both. Luckily, the software that runs the two is the same, so it doesn't really matter which iPod you have—this book will show you how all the vital stuff is done. The big difference between the two models (besides prices, colors, and so on) is that the original iPod has a Thumb Wheel plus four buttons (Play, Rewind, Menu, and Fast Forward), but when Apple introduced the mini they improved the design by doing away with the four separate buttons and adding Play, Rewind, Menu, and Fast Forward right onto the Thumb Wheel itself. What's a Thumb Wheel? You're about to find out.

So grab your iPod, turn the page, and start learning how to use the coolest digital music player ever. You're going to have a blast!

—*Stephen Gregory*

There are two iPods. This one is called just the "iPod"

> *It was the first style introduced, and it holds more songs*

The iPod comes in just one color—white—but at the time of this writing, there are three different models: one that holds 3700 songs (the 15-GB model); one that holds 5000 songs (the 20-GB model); and one that holds 10,000 songs (the 40-GB model). There is a large Thumb Wheel in the center of the iPod, with a row of four buttons above it for Rewind, Menu, Play/Pause, and Fast Forward.

> *It basically works the same—it's just smaller, less expensive, and holds fewer songs*

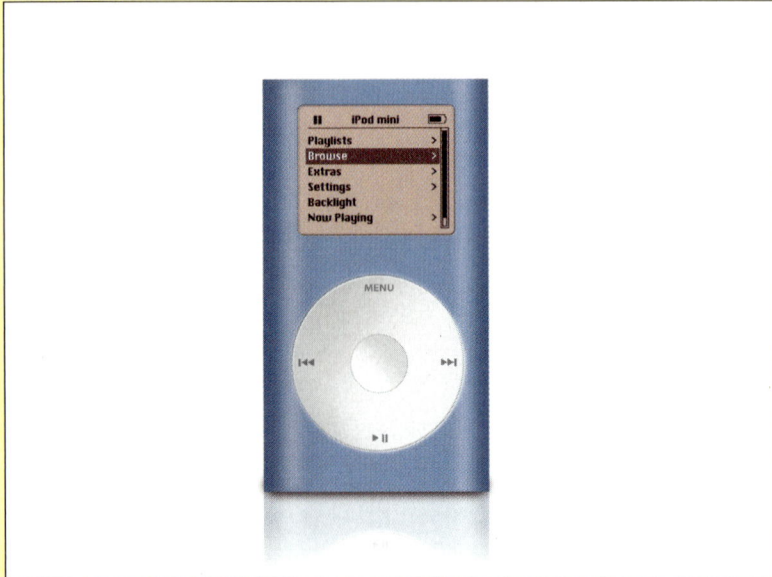

There are just a few differences between the regular iPod and the iPod mini (shown here). The most notable is that the row of buttons above the Thumb Wheel is gone; instead, the commands Menu, Rewind, Fast Forward, and Play/Pause are all incorporated right onto the wheel. The other main differences between the two models is that the iPod mini is significantly smaller in size and weight, and it comes in five colors (silver, gold, blue, pink, and green). It also hold only 1000 songs, but then again, it's less expensive than the regular iPod.

Charging your iPod's battery (using the power adapter)

> *How to plug your iPod into the wall socket for charging*

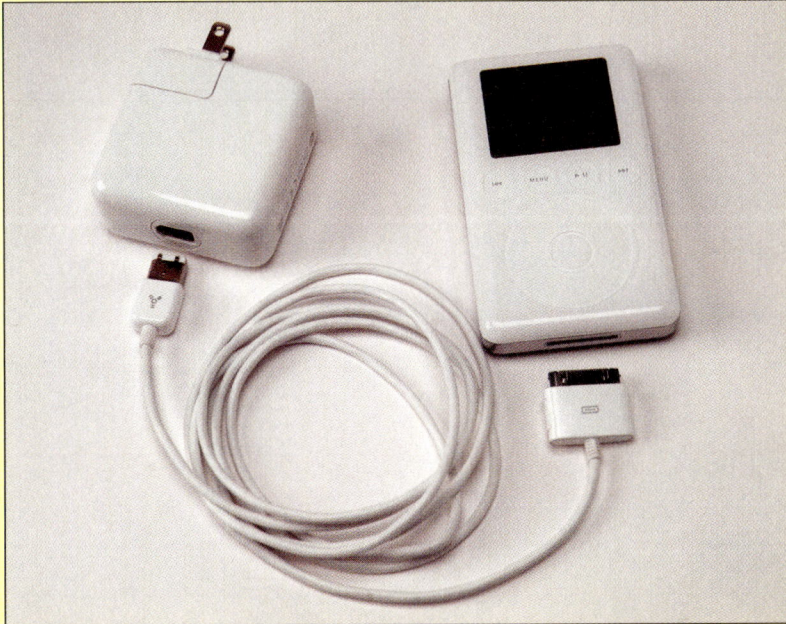

Your iPod comes with a power adapter that lets you plug your iPod directly into a standard wall socket in your home or office, so you can charge your iPod using AC power. Here's how: **Step One:** Take the FireWire cable (that comes with your iPod) and insert the thin flat side into the bottom of your iPod (there's only one slot on the bottom, so it's pretty easy to see where it goes). **Step Two:** Connect the other end of the FireWire connector to the power adapter (it comes with your iPod too!). **Step Three:** Plug your power adapter into the wall and your iPod will begin charging.

3

Charging your iPod's battery (using the Dock)

> *Just connect the Dock to your computer, and it'll charge up*

If your model of iPod didn't come with a Dock, it's one accessory that we'd recommend buying (if you bought an iPod mini, you need an iPod mini Dock). Docks are available from Apple's Web site (www.apple.com/store)* and at the time of this writing, each sold for $39.95* (plus S&H). The Dock has just one wire coming out of it (it's called a FireWire cable) and that cable connects to the FireWire port on your computer. Just put your iPod in the dock, plug your Dock into your computer, and your iPod starts charging, using the power from your computer. Another benefit is that once you connect the Dock to your computer, it automatically launches Apple's iTunes software (the link between your computer and your iPod).

*U.K. residents: £29.00. See http://store.apple.com/Apple/WebObjects/ukstore

Getting songs onto your computer

> *The iTunes music player is how you get music from your computer to your iPod*

Song Name	Time	Artist	Album	Genre	My Rai
Dude Looks like a lady.mp3	4:24	Aerosmith	Pump	Rock	★★★
The Other Side	4:06	Aerosmith	Young Lust: Aer...	Rock	★★★
Fantasy	5:05	Aldo Nova	Aldo Nova	Classic Rock	★★★
Poison	4:27	Alice Cooper			★★★
Think	3:16	Aretha Franklin	Franklin, Aretha	Soul	★★★
Turn Up The Radio	4:33	Autograph		genre	★★★
You Look Good To Me	4:51	Cherelle			★★★
Blue Jean	3:10	David Bowie			★★★
Sausalito Summer Night	5:07	Diesel	Watts in a Tank	Pop	★★★
Free Your Mind	4:52	En Vogue			★★★
Overnight Senstation	3:55	Firehouse			★★★
Stacy's Mom	3:18	Fountains of Wayne	Welcome Interst...		★★★
Sweetheart	4:11	Franke & The Knocko...	Countdown 1981	Pop	★★★
Remote Control	4:00	The Reddings			★★★

14 songs, 59.2 minutes, 60.2 MB

Before you can use your iPod, you'll need to get some songs onto it, and to do that you'll need a free copy of Apple's iTunes software (for Mac or Windows). Luckily it comes with your iPod, but if for some reason you can't find your iTunes install CD, you can download the latest version of iTunes for free from Apple's Web site (www.apple.com/itunes). iTunes itself is basically a music jukebox that lets you organize, sort, and play music on your computer. Once your songs are arranged the way you want them, you connect your iPod to your computer and then iTunes automatically copies your songs onto your iPod. So basically, iTunes and the iPod work together.

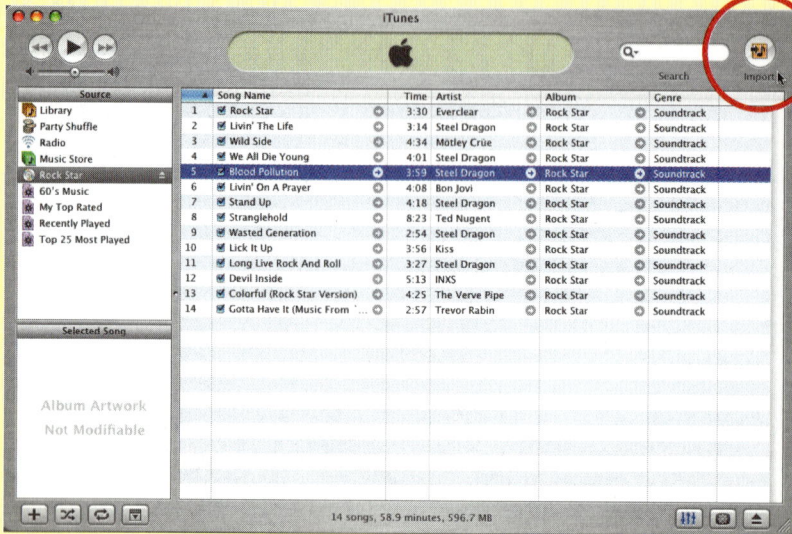

To import music from a music CD, insert the CD into your computer, then launch iTunes. The CD will appear in the Source list on the left side of the iTunes interface. Click on the CD icon, and all the music tracks (songs) on that CD will appear in the main window. If you're connected to the Internet, iTunes will automatically query an online database of songs to see if it can name the tracks for you. If it can't find the names, they'll just appear as Track 1, Track 2, etc. Click the Import button (at the top right of the iTunes window), and iTunes will convert and import all the tracks from the CD into iTunes (once this is done, you can eject the CD). Now, the next time you plug in your iPod, iTunes will copy these songs onto your iPod.

Downloading songs from the iTunes Music Store

> *Hundreds of thousands of legal music downloads are just one click away*

The world's largest source for legally downloading songs is the iTunes Music Store (ITMS for short). It reportedly has around a 70% share of the world's legal downloading market, and you can access it any time you're connected to the Internet right from within iTunes. Just click on Music Store in Source list on the left side of the iTunes interface, and it connects you (it's shown above). You can use the Search Music Store field (at the top right of the window) to find the songs you want to purchase (individual songs sell for 99¢*). Apple also has compiled lots of lists (like Celebrity lists, today's top songs, featured artists, etc.) to help you find cool music. To hear a sample of any song, just double-click directly on it.

*U.K. residents: 79p

> *How to download from legal downloading sources*

There are loads of legal music downloading services popping up every day, including sites of individual artists who are making some or all of their music downloadable (some free, some for a fee). For example, Prince (yes, Prince) has a cool site where you can download MP3s of his latest album (you can find his site at www.NPGmusicclub.com). Once you've downloaded a song, you can import it into iTunes by choosing Import from iTune's File menu. Opening a song automatically copies the song into your iTunes Library. That's it—you've downloaded a song, and now it's in your iTunes Library, ready to be transferred to your iPod (you'll see how in a moment).

Playing a song in iTunes

> *Pretend it's a cassette player, and the rest is easy*

Source	Song Name	Time	Artist	Album
Library	Dude Looks like a lady.mp3	4:24	Aerosmith	Pump
Party Shuffle	The Other Side	4:06	Aerosmith	Young Lust: Aer...
Radio	Fantasy	5:05	Aldo Nova	Aldo Nova
Music Store	Poison	4:27	Alice Cooper	
Rock Star	Think	3:16	Aretha Franklin	Franklin, Aretha
60's Music	Turn Up The Radio	4:33	Autograph	
My Top Rated	You Look Good To Me	4:51	Cherelle	
Recently Played	Blue Jean	3:10	David Bowie	
Top 25 Most Played	Sausalito Summer Night	5:07	Diesel	Watts in a Tank
	Free Your Mind	4:52	En Vogue	
	Overnight Sensation	3:55	Firehouse	

Once you've downloaded or imported some songs into iTunes, playing a song is easy—just click on the song in the main window and then click on the round Play button in the upper left corner of the iTunes interface (as circled in red above). The Play button is the one with the right-facing triangle on it (I know, you knew that, right?). To stop the song, press the Play button again (you can also start and stop the song playing by using the Spacebar on your keyboard).

9

Which song is playing right now in iTunes

> *How to find out which—and whose—song iTunes is playing*

Isn't It Time
Elapsed Time: 2:24

When you play a song within iTunes, the name of the song and artist, and the album (if available), will appear at the top center of the iTunes window. This info window also shows how long the song is, and you can have it display the Elapsed Time or Time Remaining by clicking directly on Remaining Time, Elapsed Time, or Total Time (depending on which is one is currently visible). By the way, the song name and artist is transferred over to your iPod, and when you're playing a song you'll see both displayed in the iPod window.

> *It's a two-click process*

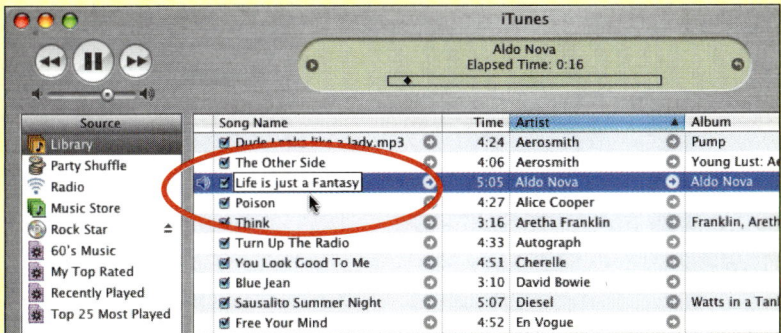

To change the name of a song in iTunes, first click on the song (to tell iTunes which song you want to edit), then click again directly on the song's name to highlight that field so you can simply type in a new name. When the new name looks right, just press the Enter key on your keyboard to lock in your new name. You can use this same technique to change the album name as well.

> *How to create custom collections of your favorite songs*

Playlists are your own custom collections of music (maybe you'd like a collection of songs to work out to, or a colletion of just mellow songs, or even a playlist of "Big Hair Bands of the 80s"). To create your own playlist just click on the plus sign (+) icon at the bottom left corner of the iTunes window (as shown here). This adds an empty playlist to the Source list on the left side of the iTunes interface, and the name field is highlighted. Name your playlist, press the Enter key on your keyboard, then drag as many songs as you like from the Library and drop them right onto your playlist to add them. Make as many different playlists as you like. When you connect your iPod, your playlists will appear under the Playlists menu.

Sorting music in iTunes

> How to put songs in the order you want them

In your "Big Hair Bands" playlist, "Life is just a Fantasy" is the first song.

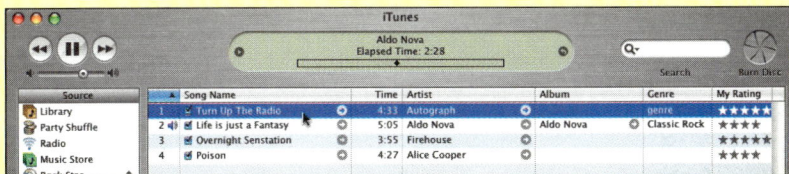

If you want "Turn Up the Radio" as the first song instead, click and drag it above "Life is just a Fantasy" (as shown here).

Once you've downloaded (or imported) songs into iTunes, you'll want to organize them in the playing order you want. When songs first come into iTunes, they appear in your Library, where iTunes sorts them alphabetically by song title, artist name, etc. If you want to organize them in the order you'd like (like your favorite song first, next favorite second, etc.), you'll need to create a playlist (see page 12), with the songs you want organize. Then click in the first column, right above the number 1 (just to the left of Song Name; now you can just click and drag the songs up (or down) the playlist to put them in the exact order you want them (as shown above).

13

Deleting songs from iTunes

> *If you don't want a particular song in your playlist, get rid of it*

If you added a song to iTunes, and then later decide you don't want it after all, just click on it and either press the Delete key (or Backspace) on your keyboard or Right-click (Mac: Control-click) on the song and choose Clear from the pop-up menu that appears (as shown above). If you delete the song from a playlist you made, that doesn't delete the song from your computer. If you do want to delete a song from your computer, then instead of going to a playlist, go to the Source list on the left side of the iTunes interface click on Library (the master list of all your songs), and delete it there—that will delete the song from your computer altogether.

Deleting an entire Playlist from iTunes

> *Tired of a particular playlist? Delete it.*

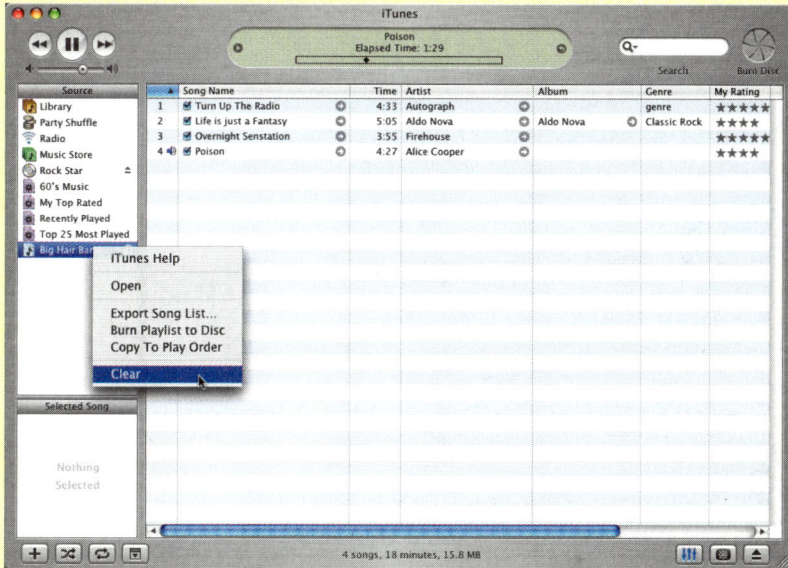

If you want to delete a playlist from iTunes, just click on that playlist in the Source list on the left side of the iTunes interface (make sure that's the one you really want to delete), then press the Delete key on your keyboard or Right-click (Mac: Control-click) on the playlist and choose Clear from the pop-up menu (as shown above). This deletes only the playlist itself—not the songs from your Library, so even though the playlist will be gone, all the songs you had in your playlist will still reside in your Library.

> ▶ **Now Playing** 🔋
>
> **1 of 254**
>
> **California Love**
>
> **Tupac & Dr. Dre**
>
> ★ ★ ★ ★ ●

Ranking songs within the iPod itself

Both iTunes and the iPod give you the ability to rank your songs (1 star being a lame song, 5 stars being a great song). The benefit of this is that you can create what are called Smart Playlists, which comprise just your top-ranked songs. To rank a song within iTunes, first click on the song to highlight it, then under the column marked "My Rating" click and drag to the right to add stars (drag to the left to remove them). Within your iPod itself, you can rank your songs while they're playing. Just press the Select button twice and the Ranking Stars window will appear (shown above). Just scroll the Thumb Wheel clockwise to add stars—and counterclockwise to take them away.

Creating Smart Playlists in iTunes

> *Let iTunes do the work of rounding up your favorite songs*

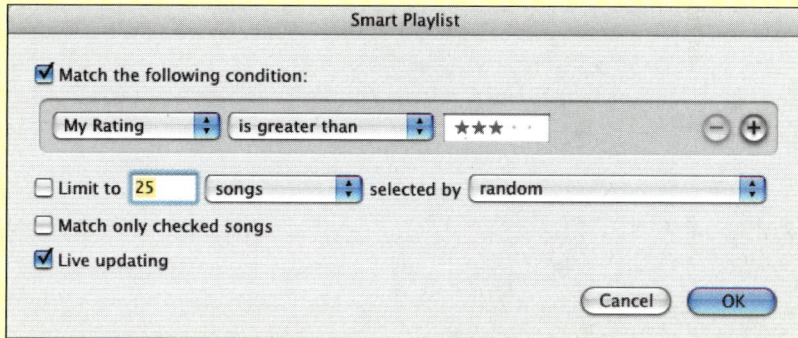

If you've been ranking your songs (using iTunes' built-in 1-to-5-star ranking system), you can have iTunes create a Smart Playlist of just your 4- and 5-star ranked songs. Here's how: In iTunes, choose New Smart Playlist from the File menu. When the dialog appears, in the first pop-up menu choose My Rating, then from the second pop-up menu choose "is greater than" and then select four stars in the third field (as shown above). Click OK and a new playlist with just your favorite songs (all 4- or 5-star ranked) will appear in the Source list. Best of all, this new Smart Playlist will transfer over to your iPod when you connect it to your computer.

Naming your iPod

When you plug in your iPod to your Mac or PC, the iPod will appear in the Source list on the left side of the iTunes interface. To rename your iPod, click on it once to select it; then just double-click directly on its name and its name field will highlight. Now you can type in your new name and press Enter on your keyboard to lock in your change.

Quick Reference

iPod

Using iPod's Controls

Use iPod's buttons and scroll pad to navigate through onscreen menus, play songs, change settings, and view information. Move your thumb along the scroll pad to highlight a menu item. Press the Select button (in the center of iPod) to select the item. Press the Menu button to go back to the previous menu.

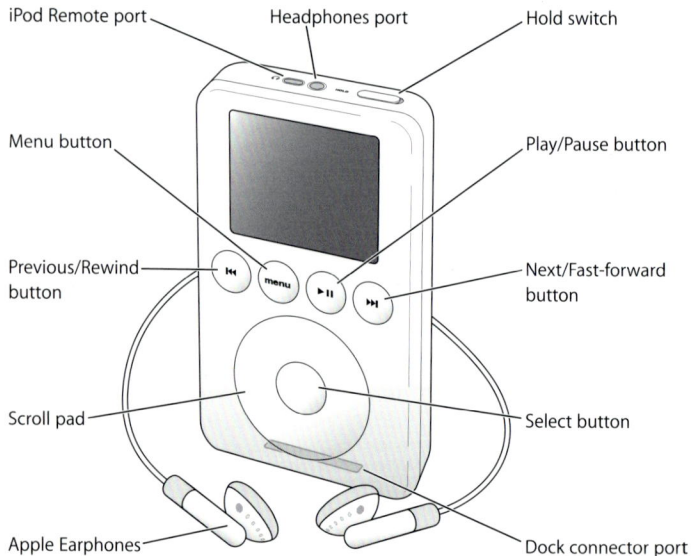

iPod Remote port

Headphones port

Hold switch

Menu button

Play/Pause button

Previous/Rewind button

Next/Fast-forward button

Scroll pad

Select button

Apple Earphones

Dock connector port

iPod Controls	
Reset iPod (For use during troubleshooting)	Toggle the Hold switch (set it to Hold, then turn it off again). Then press Menu and Play/Pause simultaneously for about 5 seconds, until the Apple logo appears.
Turn iPod on	Press any button.
Turn iPod off	Press and hold Play/Pause.
Turn the backlight on or off	Press and hold Menu or select Backlight from the main menu.
Select a menu item	Scroll to the item and press Select.
Go back to the previous menu	Press Menu.
Browse for a song	Select Playlists or Browse from the main menu.
Play a song	Highlight the song and press Select or Play/Pause.
Play all the songs in a list	Highlight the list title (an album title, or the title of a playlist, for example) and press Play/Pause.
Change the volume	From the Now Playing screen, use the scroll pad. You can also use the iPod Remote (included with some models) from any screen.
Pause a song	Press Play/Pause when no song or list is highlighted.
Disable iPod's buttons (So you don't press them accidentally)	Set the Hold switch to Hold (an orange bar appears).

iPod Controls

Skip to any point in a song	From the Now Playing screen, press Select. Then scroll to any point in the song.
Skip to the next song	Press Next/Fast-forward.
Start a song over	Press Previous/Rewind.
Play the previous song	Press Previous/Rewind twice.
Fast-forward	Press and hold Next/Fast-forward.
Rewind	Press and hold Previous/Rewind.

Printed in Taiwan

034-2296-A

Transferring songs from your computer to your iPod

> *This is the easy part—just plug your iPod into your computer*

Do not disconnect.

MENU

When songs are being transferred from your computer to your iPod, the iPod lets you know that now is not a good time to disconnect the cable.

Once you've imported all your songs into iTunes, created your own playlists, and prepared to transfer your music from your computer to your iPod, all you have to do is plug your iPod into your computer (with either a FireWire cable, a USB cable, or an iPod or iPod mini Dock). That's it. iTunes automatically transfers the songs to your iPod. It does all the work—you just connect the iPod and iTunes does the rest. When the transfer is complete, you can eject the iPod from your computer. You'll see that within the iPod's window, the "Do not disconnect" warning (shown above) is replaced with with a large check mark and "OK to disconnect."

Turning your iPod on and off

> *There is no On or Off button, so what do you do?*

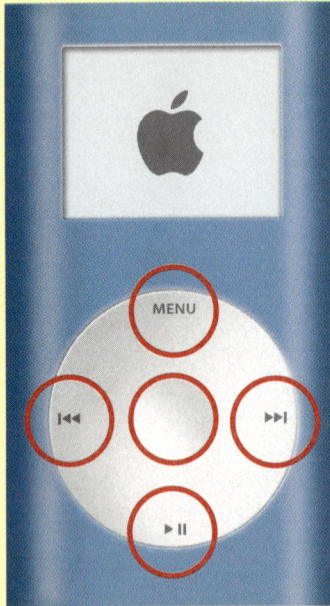

Just press any button on the front of your iPod. I wish I could make it more complicated than that, but I can't. That's it. Press any button and your iPod turns on. So basically, you can think of it this way—every button is the On button.

If you've been searching for the iPod's Off button, you'll be searching for a while; Apple decided not to include one. When you want to turn your iPod off, just hold down the Play/Pause button for a couple of seconds, and the iPod will turn itself off.

The Thumb Wheel and the Select Button

> *This is how you navigate the iPod*

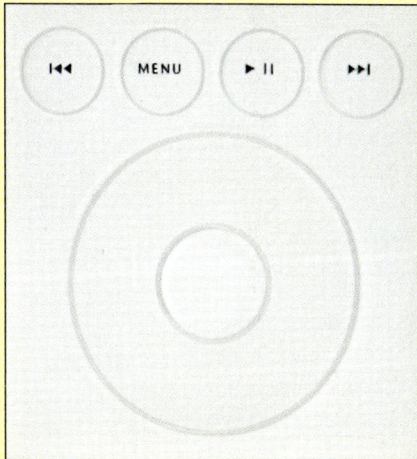

The iPod's buttons and Thumb Wheel

The iPod mini's Thumb Wheel

You find your way to songs, play them, and do just about everything else with your iPod using five buttons and a Thumb Wheel (Note: Everybody seems to call that large white circle by a different name: Touch Wheel, Scroll Wheel, Thumb Wheel, Click Wheel, Scroll Pad, etc. But for consistency's sake we're going to go with what Apple calls it on their iPod Web page—Thumb Wheel). On the original iPod, there are four separate buttons above the Thumb Wheel (as shown above left) and a fifth button (the Select button) in the center of the wheel. On the iPod mini, Apple did away with the four separate buttons and place them on the wheel itself (as shown above right), with the Select button in the center.

Using the Thumb Wheel

> *Slide to the left, slide to the right!*

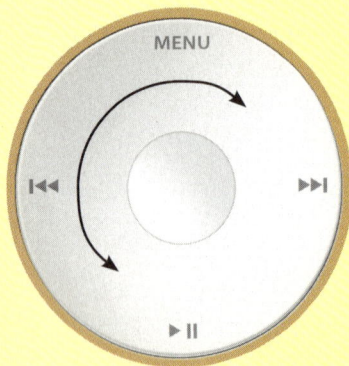

The Thumb Wheel itself doesn't slide. In fact, it doesn't move at all—it's your finger (or thumb) that's doin' the slidin' around the Thumb Wheel.

The Thumb Wheel is basically a touch pad—you lightly slide around the wheel with your finger (or thumb) in either a clockwise or counterclockwise movement. So if you're at the top of a list of songs and you want to move down the list, you lightly press your finger anywhere on the Thumb Wheel and start rotating (sliding your finger) around it in a clockwise motion. If you scrolled past the song you wanted, just backtrack—rotate counterclockwise to get back to that song. The Thumb Wheel is VERY touch-sensitive, so you don't have to press hard at all. Once you get to a song you want to play, press the Play/Pause button (or the Select button in the center).

22

Playing a song on your iPod

> *You're just one click away*

Once you've found the song you want to play, playing it is as easy as pressing one button—the Play/Pause button. I told you it was easy.

Pausing the current song

> *Want to pause for a just a moment? Here's how.*

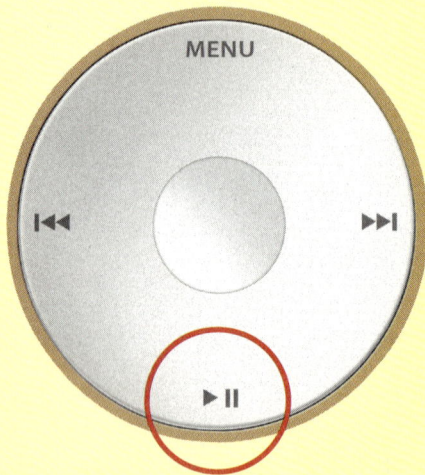

To pause the current song, just press the Play button again. To start the song again, press the Play/Pause button again. In short, for pausing and playing, hit the same button: Play/Pause.

Fast-forwarding or skipping a song

> *How to quickly get past the boring part*

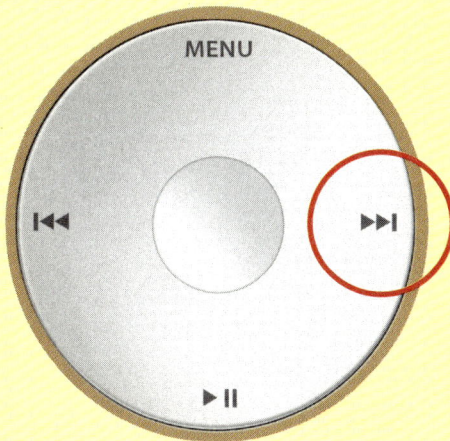

If you're listening to a song with a really long boring introduction (like the intro to Aldo Nova's "Fantasy") and you want to skip right past it and get to the screaming guitars, just press and hold on your iPod's Fast Forward button. Don't just press it once, or it'll jump to next song—you have to press and hold it to fast-forward through the song. Of course, if you do want to skip the current song entirely, just press that button once.

25

> *Want to jump ahead or backward in the currently playing song? Here's how*

```
  ▶        Now Playing        ▬▮

3 of 3170

              Reasons
      Earth Wind & Fire
   The Best of Earth, Wi...

  ▬▬▬▬▬▬▬▬▬▬▬▬▬▬▬▬▬▬▬▬▬▭
  2:00                    -2:59
```

Want to skip over a boring part of a song? Or perhaps you're trying to figure out the words to the song, and you need to hear the verse that just went by one more time? Well, you can just *Scrub* forward or backward (scrubbing is a term used by video editors that means to quickly move forward or backward while a song is playing). To scrub (jump) forward while the song is playing, just press the Select button once, then slide the Thumb Wheel in a clockwise motion. To scrub backward, slide the Thumb Wheel counterclockwise.

```
 ▶         Now Playing      ▭▶

 1 of 254


        Ai No Corrida
        Quincy Jones

   ◀■ ██████████          ◀))
```

To change the volume of the currently playing song, just press lightly on the Thumb Wheel and slide in a counterclockwise to lower the volume, and slide in a clockwise motion to raise the volume. As soon as you start sliding in either direction, your song window brings up a volume bar that shows how loud (or soft) the volume setting is. As you circle in either direction, the volume bar moves right along with you giving you a visual cue as to how loud (or soft) the volume's getting.

Getting back to the Main Menu

> *How to get quickly back to the Main Menu*

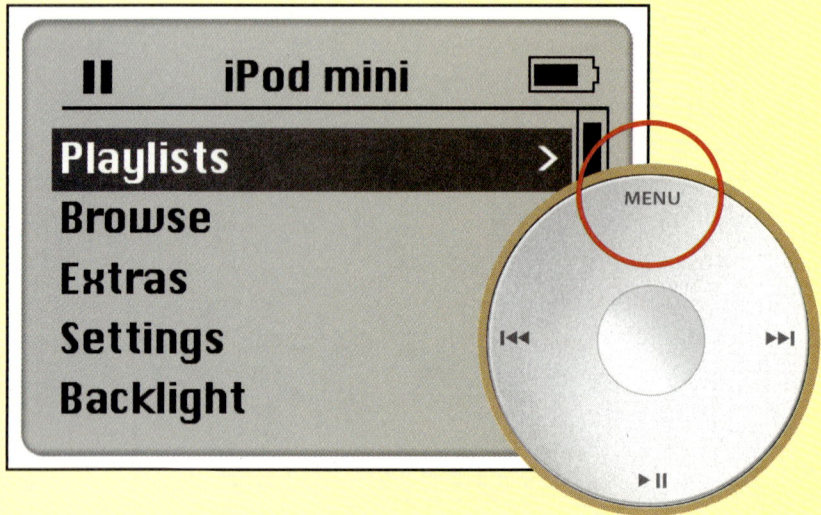

II   **iPod mini**   ▬

Playlists   **>**

Browse

Extras

Settings

Backlight

MENU

I◄◄   ►►I

►II

There are a number of different menus within the iPod interface, but since so many things happen at the Main Menu, getting back there quickly can save you lots of time. Just press the Menu button three or four times, and you'll be right there.

Playing your playlists

> *Now that you've created playlists, here's how to play them*

```
 ‖        Playlists        ▬▬▭
─────────────────────────────
 Disco Nights          >
 Mellow Mix            >
 Big Hair Rock Mix     >
 James Taylor          >
 Hip Hop Mix           >
```

To play one of the playlists on your iPod, start at the Main Menu (just press the Menu button until you see the Main Menu), then use the Thumb Wheel to scroll down to Playlists, and press the Select button in the center of the Thumb Wheel. This brings up the list of playlists on your iPod. Scroll to the playlist you want to play and press the Select button. So now you've chosen your playlist—but nothing's playing, right? That's because you have to choose a song to start with; so scroll to the song you want to start with (you can use the first song in the playlist if you like), then press the Play button (or just press the Select button again to play your song). Your iPod will now dutifully play all the songs (from the selected song forward) in your current playlist.

Playing songs in random order

> *Here's how to have your iPod shuffle the order of your songs*

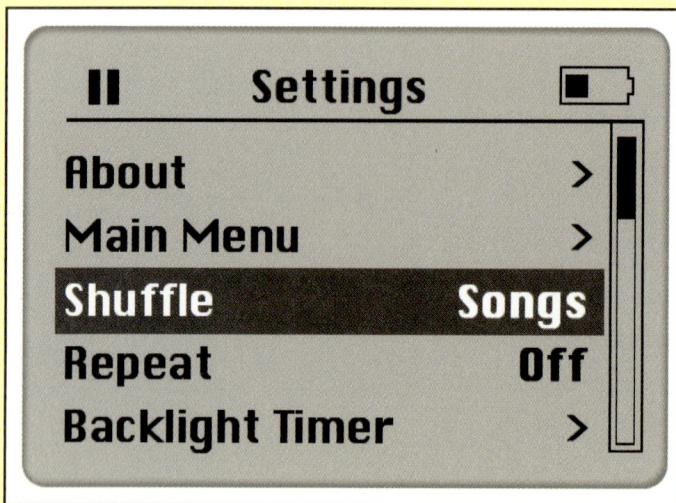

Settings

About >
Main Menu >
Shuffle **Songs**
Repeat **Off**
Backlight Timer >

By default, your iPod will play songs in your playlist in the order you have them within iTunes (for example, if you have them sorted by name, they'll play alphabetically). However, if you'd prefer they play in random order, you can turn on the iPod Shuffle feature. To turn on this random Shuffle, first go to the Main Menu. Then use the Thumb Wheel to scroll down to Settings. Press the Select button, then in the menu that appears, scroll down to Shuffle. Press the Select button once to shuffle the songs in your Playlists. To shuffle by album name, press the Select button again, and the Shuffle menu will change the order of the albums. To turn Shuffle off, press the Select button a third time.

Playing the same song over and over

> *Want to hear it again, and again, and again?*

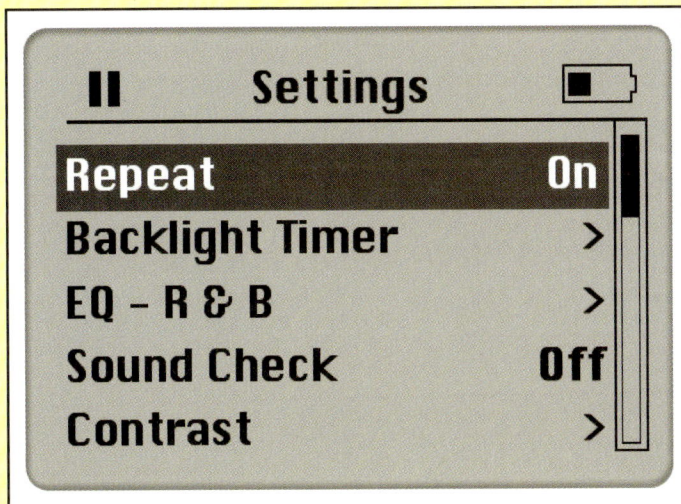

❚❚	Settings	▪️▭
Repeat		**On**
Backlight Timer		**>**
EQ – R & B		**>**
Sound Check		**Off**
Contrast		**>**

If you want to hear the same song over and over again (hey, it could happen), just go to the Main Menu and use the Thumb Wheel to scroll down to Settings. Press the Select button, then in the menu that appears scroll down to Repeat. Press the Select button once to repeat just one song over and over again (the menu will read "One"). If you want to repeat all the songs in your playlist, then press the Select button again (the menu will then read "All"). To turn Repeat off, press the Select button a third time.

Playlists

Voice Memos   >
Workout   >
Workout 30 minu...>
Workout 45 minu...>
Comedy   >
On-The-Go   >

If you're out (and by "out" I mean away from your computer), you can still create your own custom playlist from right within your iPod (as long as the songs you want in your playlist are on your iPod already). It's called an On-The-Go playlist, and to add a song to this playlist, first select the song, then press and hold down the Select button. You'll see the song blink twice, letting you know that it's been added to your On-The-Go playlist. To play the songs on your On-The-Go playlist, just go to the Main Menu, and use the Scroll Wheel to scroll down to Playlists. Press the Select button, scroll down to On-The-Go, then press the Select button to choose that playlist. Then choose any song and press the Play button.

Finding songs by browsing

> How to get to the exact song, or set of songs, you want

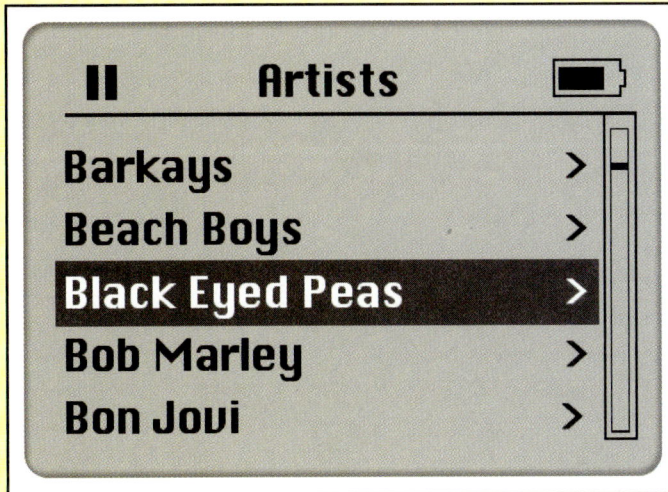

```
 ‖          Artists          ▬▬▭

 Barkays              >
 Beach Boys           >
 Black Eyed Peas      >
 Bob Marley           >
 Bon Jovi             >
```

Want to find and play just your Black Eyed Peas songs? Go to the Main Menu, use the Thumb Wheel to scroll down to Browse, and press the Select button. You can then sort (Browse) by Album, Genre, Artist, etc. To see how this works, try this: Press to select Artist and then scroll down to an artist's name. Press the Select button, and your iPod will now display only the songs on your iPod from that artist. Press the Play button and it will begin playing just those songs. This browsing feature makes sorting by Genre (like Rock songs) or Album (like *Abbey Road*, or *Damita Jo*) almost instantaneous.

Putting your iPod to sleep

> *Here's how to have your iPod turn itself off*

MENU

I◀◀   ▶▶I

▶ II

More often than not I turn my iPod off by just pressing Pause and then forgetting it. After just a minute or so of being paused, the iPod automatically turns itself off as a battery-saving measure.

Finding out how much battery time is left

iPod mini

Playlists   >
Browse   >
Extras   >
Settings   >
Backlight   >

Want to know how much of a battery charge you have left? Take a look in the upper right corner of your iPod's window, and you'll see a battery icon. If the inside of the battery icon is solid, you have a full battery. If it's half full (or half empty, depending on your personal disposition), it's got a half-charge. If it's clear, it's empty and ready for a charge-up.

If you're going to toss your iPod in your backpack, there's a reasonable chance that something in there will press against one of the buttons and start up your iPod (which will needlessly drain the battery life). So before you toss it in there (or in your pocket, or glove compartment, etc.), slide the Hold button (on the top of your iPod) to the "on" position (so the little orange area is visible, as shown above). This locks the keys and keeps anything from accidentally turning your iPod on and draining the battery. Other popular battery-saving strategies include using the buttons as little as possible (they burn battery life) and using the backlight feature sparingly (it eats up battery life big time).

*Press and hold
right here.*

MENU

I◄◄   ►►I

►II

If you're in a dark situation (meaning there's not much light where you are—not the whole "your life is in danger" thing), you can temporarily turn on your iPod's Backlight feature by pressing and holding down the Menu button for a second or two.

Setting how long the Backlight stays on

> You can set it to stay on a very short time, or long—it's up to you.

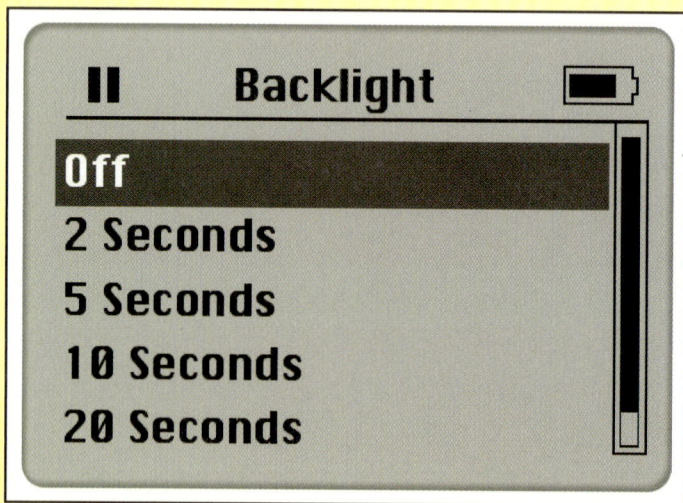

```
 ❚❚          Backlight              ▭▭▷

  Off

  2 Seconds
  5 Seconds
  10 Seconds
  20 Seconds
```

The longer the Backlight stays on, the more battery power is drained; but luckily, you can control how long the backlight feature stays on. Just press the Menu button until your see the Main Menu. Use the Thumb Wheel to scroll down to Settings, then press the Select button. Scroll down to Backlight Timer and press the Select button, and a list of times will appear. The times are listed in seconds (as shown above). Scroll to the time of your choice, then press the Select button to lock in your choice.

Customizing the Main Menu

> Set up your iPod so the options you use most appear in the Main Menu

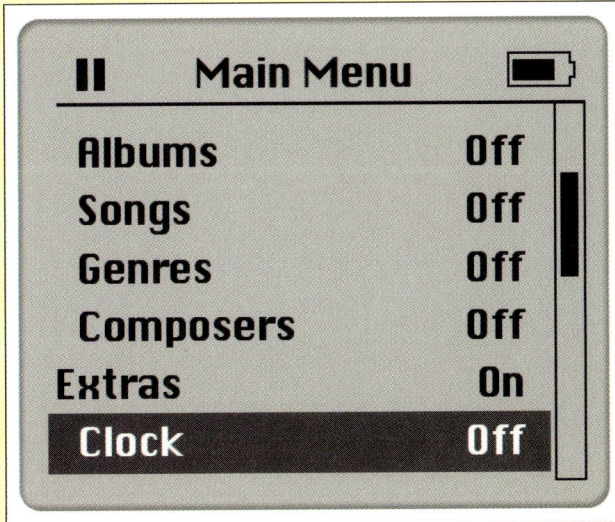

```
||      Main Menu         ▬▬▶

Albums              Off
Songs               Off
Genres              Off
Composers           Off
Extras               On
Clock               Off
```

Most recent versions of the iPod's software let you customize the items that appear in the Main Menu. That way, if you find yourself constantly digging down through different menus to get at a particular often-used feature, you can put that feature right up front. Here's how to customize your Main Menu: Start at the Main Menu and use the Thumb Wheel to scroll down to Settings, then press the Select button. Now scroll down to the menu item named Main Menu (don't go back to the Main Menu, just to the Settings menu item named Main Menu) and press the Select button. Here you'll find a list of items; you can decide which ones are visible in your real Main Menu by using the Select button to toggle between On and Off.

Updating the songs on your iPod

If you've downloaded new songs or imported songs from CDs, you'll want to get these songs into your iPod. When you connect your iPod to your Mac or PC (by using a FireWire cable, a USB cable, or a Dock), iTunes will automatically launch and update your iPod with the new songs. If you've had your iPod connected to your computer while you've added new songs to iTunes, you'll instead have to go to the iTunes File menu and choose Update Songs on iPod.

❚❚   Settings   ◼️▯

Repeat	**Off**
Backlight Timer	**>**
EQ – R & B	**>**
Sound Check	**On**
Contrast	**>**

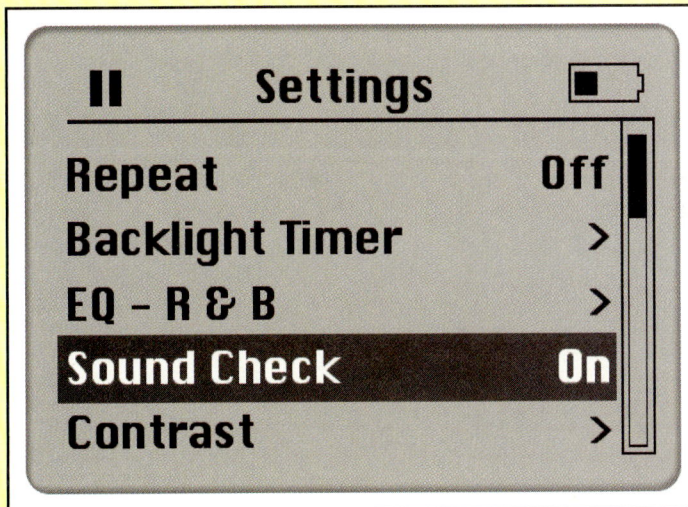

If you've ever been listening to one of your playlists and suddenly had a song come on that's so loud it nearly takes your head off, you need a "Sound Check." Sound Check is a feature that balances the overall volume from song to song, so if a song comes along that is way louder than the previous song, your iPod's Sound Check automatically tries to balance the volume so it's a smooth transition between songs. However, this cool feature is turned off by default. To turn it on, go to the Main Menu and use the Thumb Wheel to scroll down to Settings, then press the Select button. Now Scroll down to Sound Check and press the Select button to turn this ear-saving feature on.

Setting the time on your iPod

> *Hey, it beats carrying a pocketwatch*

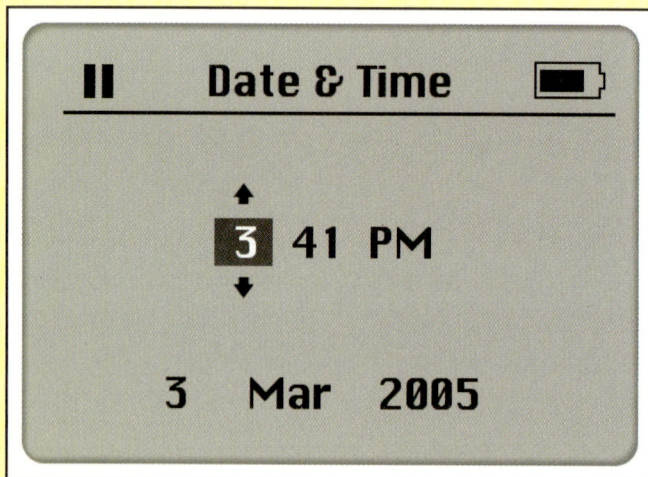

▌▌   **Date & Time**   ▰▰

3 **41 PM**

3   Mar   2005

Want to your use iPod's built-in digital clock? It's easy, plus it displays the current time while you're playing a song. First, you have to set the time. Go to the Main Menu and select Settings. In the list of settings, choose Date & Time. Use the Thumb Wheel to move the time up/down. Move from field to field by pressing the Select button. When the time is right, press Menu until you're back at the main Date & Time menu. Then, where it says Time on Menu, change the setting to On. That way, the current time will toggle into view while you're playing a song.

How to set an alarm

> *Here's how to have your iPod get your attention*

```
┃┃        Alarm Clock        ▮▭

Alarm                        Off
Time                  12:00 AM >
Sound                       Beep
```

If you're using your iPod during a workout, you might want to set an alarm so that you don't walk so long you wind up in a different area code. To set an alarm, go to the Main Menu and use the Thumb Wheel to scroll down to Extras; under Extras, select Clock. When the Clock menu appears, choose Alarm Clock. When the Alarm Clock menu appears (shown above), press the Select button to turn the alarm on. Scroll down to the Time menu and choose the time you want the alarm to sound. Lastly, scroll down to Sound and choose which sound you want the alarm to make. That's it. At the time you chose, your iPod will "sound the alarm"!

Turning off the click sound

> *It's on by default, but it doesn't have to be.*

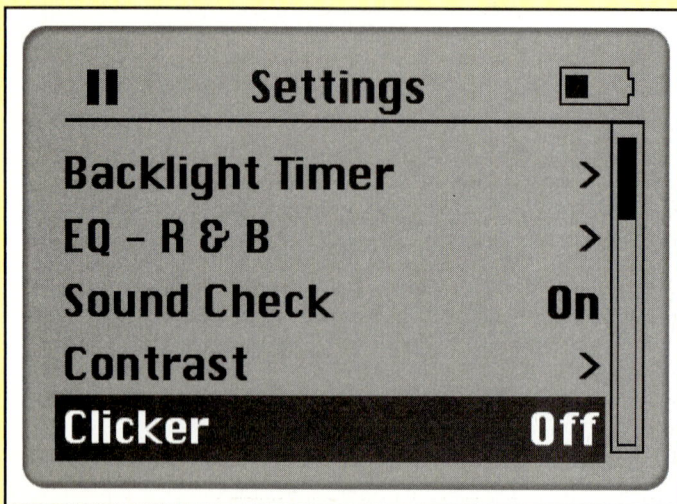

```
┃┃        Settings        ▣▭

Backlight Timer        >
EQ – R & B             >
Sound Check           On
Contrast               >
Clicker               Off
```

If you'd rather not hear that clicking sound every time you make a selection on your iPod (for example, let's say you're using your iPod at work and you're not supposed to be), you can turn off the click sound: Go to the Main Menu, scroll down and select Settings, then scroll down to Clicker. Press the Select button to turn the click sound to Off.

Setting your iPod's built-in EQ

> The default setting is Flat, which sounds just like it says—flat.

❙❙   EQ   ▧

Flat

Hip Hop

Jazz

Latin

Loudness

You can set the iPod's built-in Audio Equalizer so that the music you listen to the most sounds the best. To choose the EQ that works right for you, start at the Main Menu, use the Touch Wheel to scroll down to Settings, and press the Select button. Then scroll down to EQ and press the Select button again. This brings up a list of musical genres (like Rock, Classical, R&B, Hip Hop, Jazz, etc. Scroll to the style that fits your tastes best, and press the Select button to choose that EQ. Now put your earbuds in and listen to the difference. It's like night and day.

Finding out how many songs you can still add

> *Is there still room to add 32 more songs? Here's how to find out.*

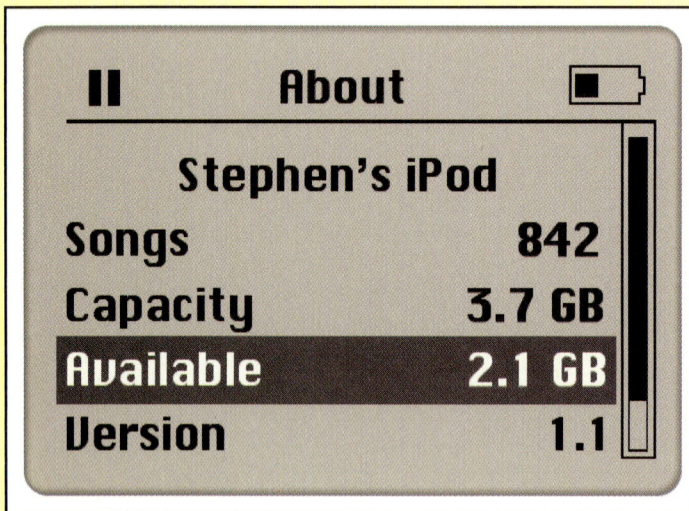

```
⏸        About         ◼▭

      Stephen's iPod
  Songs            842
  Capacity      3.7 GB
  Available     2.1 GB
  Version          1.1
```

If you want to know how much room is left on your iPod (so you can add more songs), just go to the Main Menu, use the Touch Wheel to scroll down to Settings, and press the Select button. Then scroll to About and press the Select button again. This brings up a readout of how many songs are on your iPod, how much disk space they take up, and how much space is left for adding new songs. If you're using MP3s, 32 songs would take up approximately 130 MB of your drive space (at about 4 MB per song), so if you had 2.1 GB free, you could add up to around 500 more songs. If you're using higher-quality AAC files, 32 songs (at roughly 5 MB apiece) would take 160 MB, and with 2.1 GB free, you could add up to just over 400 songs.

Setting your LCD screen contrast

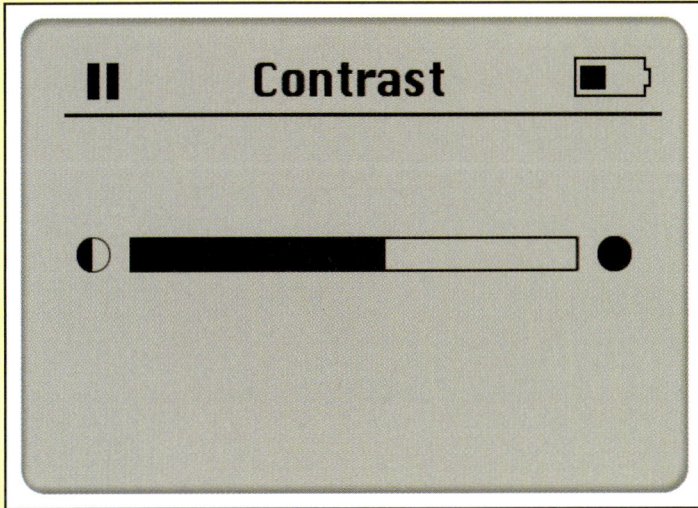

If you use your iPod outdoors a lot, you may want to increase the amount of contrast for your iPod's LCD display window so the menus are easier to read. To adjust the contrast, start at the Main Menu, use the Touch Wheel to scroll down to Settings, and then click the Select button. Then scroll down to Contrast and click the Select button again. This brings up the Contrast slider bar. By default the amount of contrast is set right in the middle. To add more contrast (making the display easier to read in bright light), move the Touch Wheel to the right (clockwise). If you go too far, you can reduce the amount of contrast by scrolling the Touch Wheel to the left (counterclockwise).

Playing the iPod's built-in games

> *You didn't know the iPod had games? Don't get excited—they're not that great.*

⏸ Games 🔋

Brick ❯

Music Quiz ❯

Parachute ❯

Solitaire ❯

Got a full battery and some time to kill? Try some of the iPod's built-in games. To find them, go to the Main Menu and use the Thumb Wheel to scroll down to Extras, then press the Select button. Next scroll down to Games and press the Select button to reveal the four built-in games: Brick (kind of like the old Breakout video game); Music Quiz (just what it sounds like); Parachute (kind of a bad version of the old Missile Command game); and Solitaire (which isn't terribly bad, but it is terribly small). Press the Select button to choose the game of your choice, then press Select again to start the game. Then watch the hours just fly by.

Deleting a song from your iPod

> *What to do when you really hate a particular song*

iPod Preferences

○ Automatically update all songs and playlists
○ Automatically update selected playlists only:

☐ 60's Music
☐ My Top Rated
☐ Recently Played
☐ Top 25 Most Played
☐ Big Hair Bands

◉ Manually manage songs and playlists

☑ Open iTunes when attached
☑ Enable disk use
☐ Only update checked songs

(Cancel) (OK)

If a song you really hate winds up sneaking its way onto your iPod (this sometimes happens with a song you liked at one time but that really starts to get on your nerves after a few dozen times), you can delete the song. The easiest way is to just delete the song from your iTunes playlist, then plug in your iPod to your computer, and when it updates, the offending song it gone! If you want to do it the hard way, connect your iPod to your computer, then click on the iPod Preferences button at the bottom right corner of the iTunes window. Then click on "Manually manage songs and playlists" (as shown above). In iTunes, click on your iPod, scroll down to the song you want to delete, click it, then press the Delete key on your keyboard. That removes it from your iPod, but not from iTunes.

If Your iPod won't turn on

> *If it's not out of battery power, here's what to try next—resetting your iPod*

If you just can't get your iPod to come on, first check to see if your button lock is turned on (that's the Hold button on the top of your iPod that, when engaged, keeps buttons from being pressed accidentally). Slide the button over so you don't see the orange indicator any longer, then try your iPod again. If it still doesn't work, maybe it's the battery—try plugging the iPod into the wall using the AC power adapter. If neither of these methods works, you can reset your iPod by sliding the Hold button over to the Lock position, and then unlock it again. Now hold down both the Play button and the Menu button at the same time (NOTE: If you have an iPod mini, instead hold down both the Menu button and the Select button, as shown above) until you see the Apple logo appear in the LCD window; then release both buttons.

Where to find iPod accessories

> *Apple sells more cool add-ons than you can stick a shake at.*

Apple - iPod - Cool Accessories

http://www.apple.com/ipod/accessories.html ⊙ ⚬ Q⟡ Google

Accessories for iPod users on the go

InMotion Portable iPod Speakers
The first powered audio system designed exclusively for the iPod, Altec Lansing's ultra-portable, battery-operated stereo speaker system delivers a full spectrum of pure, rich sound. Works with all iPods.

iPod mini Arm Band
Take your iPod mini on your next hike, go jogging or run errands. The lightweight Arm Band keeps your iPod mini secure and lets you conveniently adjust volume and select songs and playlists.

In-Ear Headphones
These headphones feature great sound quality and bass response, as well as enhanced sound. With three differenet sized caps, you get a snug comfortable fit for ears big and small.

Belkin Voice Recorder
Record voice notes on your iPod with the Belkin Voice Recorder. You can record memos, meetings, interviews and more and store them on your iPod, which stamps them with the date and time. (Not compatible with iPod mini.)

iPod Remote and Earbuds
Listening to your iPod on the go is even more convenient with this wired remote and extra set of earphones. Works with iPod with dock connector and iPod mini.

Belkin Media Reader
Save a bundle on memory cards the next time you take your digital camera on vacation. When your card is full, transfer the images to your iPod via the handy Belkin Media Reader. (Not compatible with iPod mini.)

Belkin Battery Pack
Away from your computer for a few days? Belkin's optional backup battery pack gives you more than 20 hours of battery life on four standard AA batteries.

iPod Carrying Case
Protect your iPod from the elements and enhance its portability with this custom-made carrying case that clips to your belt, purse or backpack.

World Travel Adapter Kit
With the addition of this kit, iPod goes anywhere in the world. Includes six AC plugs with prongs that fit different electrical outlets around the world.

Apple apparently wants you to have cool iPod accessories, because it makes getting them so easy. The company has a large collection of iPod and iPod mini accessories (everything from wireless controllers to iPod arm bands for joggers) at the Apple online store at www.apple.com/ipod/accessories.*

*U.K. residents see http://store.apple.com/Apple/WebObjects/ukstore

51

Index

accessories, 4, 51
Alarm Clock, 43
Backlight feature, 37–38
battery, 3–4, 35, 36
click sound, 44
date and time, 42
disk space, 1, 2, 46
Dock, 4
downloading
  iTunes, 5
  songs, 7–8
Equalizer (EQ), 45
fast forward, 1, 25
Firewire cable, 3, 4
games, 48
importing songs from
  CD, 6
iPod. See also playlists;
  songs
  accessories, 4, 51
  Alarm Clock, 43
  Backlight feature, 37–38
  battery, 3–4, 35–36
  click sound, 44
  date and time, 42
  deleting songs, 49
  disk space, 1, 2, 46
  Equalizer (EQ), 45
  finding songs on, 33
  games, 48
  Main Menu, 28, 39
  models of, 1, 2
  naming, 18

Preferences for, 49
  resetting, 50
  screen contrast for, 47
  Thumb Wheel, 1, 21–22
  transferring songs to, 19
  turning off, 20, 34
  turning on, 20, 50
  volume, 27, 41
iTunes
  changing song name, 11
  deleting songs, 14
  downloading newest, 5
  getting new songs, 40
  launching, 4
  name of song playing, 10
  playlists, 12, 17
  sorting songs, 13
iTunes Music Store, 7
names
  changing song, 11
  finding out song's, 10
  naming your iPod, 18
pause, 24
playlists
  creating, 12
  deleting, 15
  On-The-Go, 32
  playing, 29
  Smart, 17
Power Adapter, 3
ranking songs, 16
repeating songs, 31
screen contrast, 47

scrubbing through
  songs, 26
skipping songs, 25
sleep mode, 34
smart playlists, 17
songs. See also playlists
  deleting, 14, 49
  disk space for, 1, 2, 46
  downloading, 6–8
  fast forwarding, 1, 25
  finding, 33
  getting new, 40
  importing from CD, 6
  information about, 10
  pausing, 24
  playing, 9, 23
  ranking, 16
  renaming, 11
  repeating, 31
  scrubbing through, 26
  shuffling order of, 30
  skipping, 25
  sorting, 13
  transferring to iPod, 19
  volume, 27, 41
sorting songs, 13
Thumb Wheel, 1, 21–22
turning off
  click sound, 44
  iPod, 20, 34
turning on iPod, 20, 50
volume, 27, 41